C00 376 169X

KU-239-953

Looking at Small Mammals

The Weasel Family

Sally Morgan

Chrysalis Children's Books

First published in the UK in 2004 by
Chrysalis Children's Books
An imprint of Chrysalis Books Group Plc
The Chrysalis Building, Bramley Road
London W10 6SP

Copyright © Chrysalis Books Plc 2004
Text copyright © Sally Morgan 2004

Editorial manager: Joyce Bentley
Series editor: Debbie Foy
Editors: Clare Lewis, Joseph Fullman
Designer: Wladek Szechter
Picture researcher: Sally Morgan
Illustrations: Woody

All rights reserved. No part of this book may be
reproduced or utilized in any form or by any means,
electronic or mechanical, including photocopying,
recording or by any information storage and retrieval
system, without written permission from the publisher,
except by a reviewer who may quote passages in review.

ISBN 1 84458 101 2

Printed in China

10 9 8 7 6 5 4 3 2 1

British Library Cataloguing in Publication Data for this
book is available from the British Library.

Picture acknowledgements:
Ecoscene: 7T & 7B Peter Cairns; 19T Anthony
Cooper; 9T Clive Druett; 21B William Middleton; 4,
21T Jack Milchanowski; 3, 32 Neeraj Mishra; 1, 9B,
13, 14, 17, 23, 24, 27B Robert Pickett; 15B, 19B, 26
John Pitcher; 27T Fritz Polking; 5T, 5B, 6, 10, 11T &
11B, 15T, 20, 25 Robin Redfern; 22 Alan Towse. Front
cover: TCL Jack Milchanowski; B Robert Pickett; TL,
TCR, TR, CL, CR Robin Redfern. Back cover: TCL
Jack Milchanowski; TL, TCR, TR, Robin Redfern.
Rex Features: 2, 16 Ellen Thornell (ETL). Still
Pictures: 18 Fritz Polking.

HOMEWORK SUPPORT

DUNDEE CITY
COUNCIL

LOCATION
KIRKTON

ACCESSION NUMBER
COO 376 169X

SUPPLIER
SCB

£10·99

CLASS No.
599·76

8·2·05

Contents

What are weasels?

Weasels belong to a group of animals called **mammals**. Most mammals have four legs and are covered in hair. They give birth to live young. Young mammals feed on their mother's milk for the first weeks of their lives.

The long-tailed weasel is covered in thick fur which keeps it warm in winter.

The otter is well suited to living in water with its waterproof coat and webbed paws.

The weasel family is large and includes many different animals such as stoats, pine martens, polecats, skunks and otters. Weasels are related to dogs, bears and racoons.

The slender-bodied mink, a close relative of the stoat, lives by water.

The weasel family

Most weasels have long bodies and short legs. Their bodies are covered in thick fur. The colour of their fur is usually brown but some have white spots or stripes. Their feet end in five toes, which have curved claws.

The weasel has a small, flattened head, no wider than its neck, so it can put its head down mouse holes.

The wolverine is a bear-like animal that has extremely powerful jaws to crunch through deer bones.

Their ears are short. Members of the weasel family vary in size. The smallest is the weasel and the largest are giant otters and wolverines.

The Eurasian badger has a small pointed head with black and white stripes.

7

Where do weasels live?

Weasels and their relatives are found in most areas of the world. However, they are not found in Australia, New Zealand or in Antarctica.

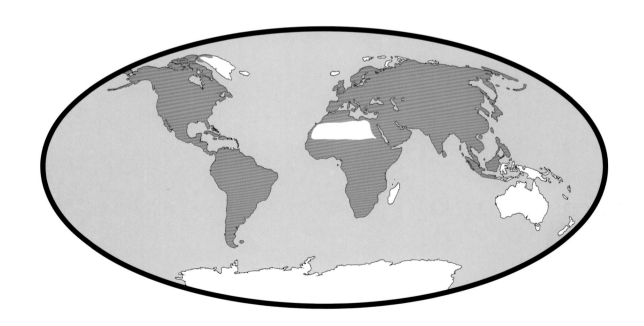

The areas shaded in pink on this map of the world show where weasels live.

Otters are mostly solitary animals that hunt along rivers.

The stoat lives in woodlands and on farmland. Some are found in gardens.

Most weasels live on land. They can be found in woodlands, on farmland and in gardens and parks. Otters and minks live by rivers and sea otters swim in the ocean.

9

What do weasels eat?

This small weasel has managed to kill a rabbit many times larger than itself.

The members of the weasel family are **carnivores.** This means they eat meat. They hunt and kill other animals for food. Badgers eat a variety of foods including worms, beetles, roots and fruits.

Minks are excellent swimmers. This mink has caught a large river fish.

Carnivores have sharp teeth and claws which they use to catch their **prey**. They have large teeth at the back of their mouths that slice through meat and crunch bone. Weasels and stoats may be small but they will attack large animals such as birds and rabbits.

Polecats will eat almost anything they can catch, such as this pigeon.

Finding food

Weasels find their food using their senses. They have good eyesight to spot their prey moving in the **undergrowth**.

By standing on its hind legs, a stoat can get a better view of its surroundings.

12

Often they hunt at night. They need good senses of smell and hearing to find prey in the dark. They have long hairs called **whiskers** around their mouths. Whiskers help the animal to feel its way in the dark.

There is a cluster of whiskers around the nose of this Asian short-clawed otter.

Getting around

Weasels and stoats can run quickly over the ground. They have a slim body that can squeeze through small gaps. The pine marten can climb trees and leap

Members of the weasel family, including this American fisher, have five toes on each foot.

14

The cat-like pine marten can leap from branch to branch. It is the most agile of the weasel family.

from branch to branch. The otter and the mink are excellent swimmers and can catch fish in the water. They are also fast when they run over land.

The American mink's feet are partly webbed to help it swim.

Smelly animals!

Smell is very important to the weasel family.

Most live and hunt in one particular area.

This area is called a **territory**. They mark

the edge of their territory

with their own smell.

Weasels and stoats live alone and mark the boundaries of their territories to warn others away.

When threatened a skunk fluffs its fur and lifts its tail. If the threat does not go away it will turn around and spray a jet of smelly liquid.

For example, some rub their body against a tree trunk or fence. Others produce a smelly substance that they leave on the ground. The smell is a message for others to stay away! Skunks, polecats and zorillas use smell to protect themselves. For example, if a skunk is attacked, it turns around and sprays a foul-smelling liquid over its attacker!

17

Living by the river

Otters and minks live by the river. Both have a long body and tail. Their fur is **waterproof**. They have webbed feet to help them swim.

An otter holds its prey firmly in its paws while it eats.

The long, slender shape of the otter is perfect for swimming through water.

Otters and minks feed on fish and frogs.

Minks also eat birds and small mammals.

Otters dig out **burrows** in the riverbank. The burrow is called a **holt**. The female otter gives birth to two or three cubs in her holt.

Young minks stay with their mother for about four months before leaving her to live on their own.

19

Badgers

Badgers are larger animals than stoats and weasels. Most have a small head and a powerful body. Badgers have long claws, which are ideal for digging. Some badgers dig a large burrow in the ground called a **sett**.

A family of badgers emerge from their sett at night to hunt for food.

The American badger often leaves its burrow to hunt during the day.

The long claws on the front feet of the badger are used to rip through soil.

There are several different types of badger. Eurasian and American badgers have a white stripe on their head. The Eurasian badger is **nocturnal**. This means it sleeps in its burrow during the day and comes out to feed at night.

Baby weasels

Most of the weasel family dig a burrow in which they make their nest. They give birth to tiny babies that are covered in fur.

Ferrets and polecats give birth to between three and six babies, called kits.

This young mink will feed on its mother's milk for about the first ten weeks of its life.

Their eyes are closed for about the first ten days. Weasels and stoats may have as many as seven babies while otters give birth to only two or three young.

Big relatives

Weasels and stoats have some large relatives, including bears, wolves and coyotes. These relatives are carnivores too. The brown bear is the world's largest land-living carnivore.

Two young brown bear cubs follow their mother. Brown bears in North America are called grizzly bears.

Two polar bears use their sharp
teeth and claws to rip open the
body of a seal.

The call of the coyote is a series
of yelps followed by a long wail
that sounds like a siren.

Bears have large teeth and long sharp claws which they use to catch their prey.

The polar bear is found in the Arctic. It has thick white fur to keep it warm. It feeds on seals and small whales. The wolf looks like a large dog and lives and hunts in groups called packs.

Investigate!

Watching weasels

Many people may be lucky enough to have weasels, stoats and badgers in their garden or local park. Some people keep ferrets as pets. You could visit a zoo or wildlife park where you can see members of the weasel family close up. You can also learn more about weasels by reading about them in books or searching on the Internet.

Paw prints

If snow is on the ground you may be able to see the tracks of animals. You may not be able to find paw prints of weasels or badgers but, in some areas, you could find tracks of dogs or even coyotes or wolves. Try and answer these questions. How many toes are there? Can you see the claws? How big are the paw prints? How far apart are the individual paw prints?

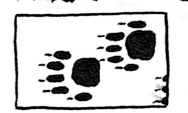

See if you can spot a badger sett while out in the woods, but be careful not to disturb the badgers!

Badger signs

Look out for badger setts when you are out with your family in local woods. One clue to finding a badger sett is a pile of freshly dug soil around a large hole in the ground. Sometimes there will be several holes. Badgers dig worms and other small animals from the soil using their claws. Look around the sett to see if you can find scrapings in the ground. If you do find a sett be careful that you do not disturb the badgers.

Look out for dogs' footprints in your local park. Compare them to the footprint of a weasel or badger.

Weasel facts

✓ Don't stand too close to a skunk. When attacked, the skunk does a handstand and sprays a jet of foul-smelling liquid over a distance of more than three metres!

✓ The wolverine is a large bear-like weasel that lives in the frozen north. Its powerful jaws can crunch through frozen meat and bone that it finds in the snow.

✓ The weasel has to eat one-third of its body weight every day, just to stay alive.

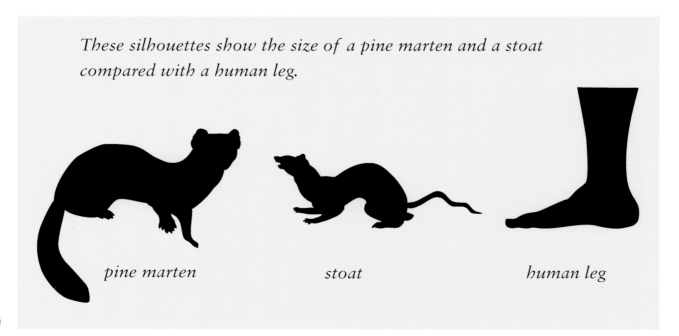

These silhouettes show the size of a pine marten and a stoat compared with a human leg.

pine marten　　　*stoat*　　　*human leg*

Glossary

burrow a large hole or tunnel in the ground.

carnivore an animal that eats other animals.

holt the name given to an otter's home.

mammal an animal that feeds their young with milk and is covered in fur.

nocturnal active at night, sleeps during the day.

prey an animal that is hunted by other animals.

sett the name given to a badger's home.

territory an area in which an animal lives and hunts.

undergrowth low growing plants on the ground, usually under trees.

waterproof a covering that keeps water out, for example, the fur of an otter.

webbed having flaps of skin between the toes.

whisker stiff hair found around the mouth and nose of a mammal.

Index